In the NAME *of* JESUS

In the NAME *of* JESUS

by DAVID K. BERNARD

In the Name of Jesus

by David K. Bernard

©1992 David K. Bernard
Printing History: 1994, 1995, 1998

Cover Design by Tim Agnew

All Scripture quotations in this book are from the King James Version of the Bible unless otherwise identified.

All right reserved. No portion of this publication may be reproduced, stored in an electonic system, or transmitted in any form or by any means, electronic, mechanical, photocopy, recording, or otherwise, without the prior permission of Word Aflame Press. Brief quotations may be used in literary reviews.

Printed in United States of America

Printed by

WORD AFLAME®PRESS
8855 DUNN ROAD
HAZELWOOD, MO 63042-2299

Bernard, David K. 1956—
   In the name of Jesus / David K. Bernard.
     p. cm.
   ISBN 0-932581-95-1
   1. God—Name. 2. Jesus Christ—Name. 3. Baptism in the name of Jesus.
4. Oneness Pentecostal churches—Doctrines. I. Title.
   BT180.N2B47 1992
   232--dc20   91-38203
                                                                                   CIP

*To
Grannie
and
Papa*

Contents

Preface 9
1. People of the Name 11
2. The Significance of God's Name 19
3. Call His Name Jesus 29
4. Yahweh, Yashua, or Jesus? 35
5. Baptism in the Name of Jesus 41
6. The Baptismal Formula according
   to Matthew 28:19 55
7. The Baptismal Formula and the Greek Text . 71

Notes 83

Preface

The doctrine of the name of God is an exciting yet sometimes neglected subject. This book investigates the biblical significance of God's name and specifically the name of Jesus. It also discusses the importance of invoking the name of Jesus in water baptism.

Much of this material previously appeared in article form: chapter 1 in the *Pentecostal Herald*, August 1990; chapter 3 in the *Pentecostal Herald*, December 1986; chapter 4 in the *Pentecostal Herald*, October 1988; and chapter 7 partially in the *Pentecostal Herald*, February 1987, and partially in the *Forward*, October–December 1986. Some of the articles were modified or expanded slightly for this book.

I pray that this book will encourage a fresh appreciation for the majesty of "our great God and Savior Jesus Christ" (Titus 2:13, NKJV) and for the privilege that we have to be "a people for his name" (Acts 15:14).

1

People of the Name

God at the first did visit the Gentiles, to take out of them a people for his name (Acts 15:14).

The note on the windshield of my car read, "Would you take me to your church?" I did not recognize the name and telephone number at the bottom, but I called the number and arranged transportation for the girl who had made the request.

Like me, she was a student at the University of Texas at Austin, and she was searching for God. While visiting a friend of hers at the apartment complex where I lived, she had been attracted by the bumper sticker on my car that said: "PEOPLE OF THE NAME . . . JESUS" and in small letters, "United Pentecostal Church." As a result of that contact, she is a member of a United Pentecostal Church today.

One day as I was driving the same car down a freeway in Houston, someone behind me began honking his horn insistently. I looked back to see the driver pointing repeatedly toward the top of his car with a big grin on his face. It took me a while to realize that he had read my bumper sticker and wanted me to know that he too was one of those "People of the Name" who served the one true God.

On another occasion, as I drove along a road that had various places of worldly entertainment—bars, a massage parlor, an "adult" bookstore, a movie theater —a temptation came to me. The devil seemed to say, "If you were to go into one of these places, no one would recognize you. You could have fun and never get caught." Immediately I thought of my bumper sticker and a question came to mind: If people saw my car parked at one of these places what would they think of my church and, most of all, my Lord? Of course, the true motivation and power to resist temptation that day did not come from the name on the bumper sticker, but from the Bearer of that name, who dwelt in my heart by His Spirit.

On these three occasions and others like them, my bumper sticker served as a mark of identification to an inquirer, to another Christian, and to myself. Even so, the name of Jesus identifies us to the world, to fellow believers, and to ourselves. God's people have always been identified by His name.

In the Old Testament

In the Old Testament God established a covenant with the nation of Israel. If they would serve Him, He promised to establish them, make them a holy people, bless them greatly, and make them a witness of Him to all nations, and He expressed this plan by identifying them with His name Jehovah. (In the King James Version and New King James Version, LORD, in large and small capitals, stands for the name Yahweh in the Hebrew text, also known in English as Jehovah.)

Thus Moses proclaimed, "The LORD [Jehovah] shall command the blessing upon thee in thy storehouses, and in all that thou settest thine hand unto; and he shall bless thee in the land which the LORD thy God giveth thee. The LORD shall establish thee an holy people unto himself, as he hath sworn unto thee, if thou shalt keep the commandments of the LORD thy God, and walk in his ways. And all people of the earth shall see that thou art called by the name of the LORD; and they shall be afraid of thee" (Deuteronomy 28:8-10).

Throughout the Old Testament, God identified His people as those who were called by His name (II Chronicles 7:14; Isaiah 43:5-7; Daniel 9:19). God's name represents His character, power, authority, and presence (Exodus 3:13-14; 6:3-8; 9:16; 23:20-21; I Kings 8:27-29). To be called by His name means to be identified with Him, to know His divine character, to experience His miraculous power, to live under His sovereign authority, and to dwell in His sacred presence. God's name represents God Himself; it is God in self-revelation.

Thus God's people exalt His name (Psalm 34:3). They praise and bless His name (Psalm 113:1-3). They seek His name and call upon His name (Psalm 83:16; 105:1). They sanctify His name, treating it as holy, revered, and sacred by the way they use it and also by the way they live (Isaiah 29:23). By word and deed they declare his name to each other and to the world (Psalm 22:22).

Those who fear (respect, revere) God's name and love God's name have a great inheritance (Psalm 61:5; 69:36). Those who remember His name have an unfailing source of strength and protection (Psalm 20:7; Proverbs 18:10). God reserves blessings for those who think on His name (Malachi 3:16).

The faith, commitment, and holiness of God's true people in the Old Testament can be summed up in the words of Micah 4:5: "We will walk in the name of the LORD our God for ever and ever."

In the New Testament

The New Testament church continued to exalt God's name, the only difference being that they had a greater revelation of God and His name. The God of the Old Testament—Jehovah—had manifested Himself in flesh to be the Savior, and the name by which He chose to come was Jesus, which literally means Jehovah-Savior. (See Matthew 1:21, 23.) Thus the name of Jesus is the only saving name (Acts 4:12), the highest name ever made known (Philippians 2:9), and the name by which the New Testament church is identified.

God united both Jews and Gentiles into His church, thereby establishing a people of the name of Jesus (Acts 15:14). New Testament believers have the name of Jesus invoked over them (Acts 15:17; James 2:7).

Jesus instructed His disciples to gather in His name (Matthew 18:20), to pray in His name (John 14:13-14), and to preach in His name (Luke 24:47). He said they would cast out demons, receive divine protection, and receive healings in His name (Mark 16:17-18), as well as receive the Holy Spirit in His name (John 14:26). He also warned that they would be reviled, persecuted, and hated for His name's sake (Matthew 5:11; 10:22).

After the New Testament church was founded on the Day of Pentecost, the believers went forth in the name of Jesus. They baptized by invoking the name of Jesus (Acts 2:38; 8:16; 10:48; 19:5; 22:16). They prayed for the sick and received healings by invoking the name of Jesus (Acts 3:6, 16; 4:10; James 5:14). They cast out demons by invoking the name of Jesus (Acts 16:18). They taught and preached everywhere in His name (Acts 5:28, 40, 42). They called on His name (Acts 9:21), labored for His name (Revelation 2:3), held fast to His name (Revelation 2:13), and refused to deny His name (Revelation 3:8). In fact, they proclaimed that salvation was only in the name of Jesus (Acts 4:12).

They lived a holy life in order to bear witness of His name (II Timothy 2:19). They bore His name to the world, and they suffered for His name (Acts 9:15-16). They were reproached for His name (I Peter 4:14), and they even risked their lives for His name (Acts 15:26). When persecuted, they rejoiced "that they were counted worthy to suffer shame for his name" (Acts 5:41). They did not enjoy beatings, imprisonment, deprivation, and martyrdom any more than we do, but they rejoiced that even their enemies identified them with Jesus.

The People of the Name Today

Strangely, much of Christendom does not teach the doctrine of the name of God, and many professing Christians seem reluctant to be identified totally with the name of Jesus. Instead, they seem to regard the supreme name of God as unimportant, unknowable, or described by trinitarian titles.

Some of them even attack or ridicule Oneness Pentecostals for our devotion to the name of Jesus. Some call us "Jesus Only" as a term of disparagement. (The label originated because we baptize in the name of Jesus only, but some apply it to us in an attempt to say that we deny God as the Father and the Holy Spirit.) In Central America we are often ridiculed by other groups as the "Jesusites."

Significantly, even when others revile or persecute us, they identify us with Jesus. We can rejoice that even when their intent is to discredit us, they nevertheless recognize our devotion to the name of Jesus. One observer joked that we should not be called "Jesus Only" but "Jesus Everything." Another trinitarian observer remarked publicly, "No one loves and exalts Jesus more than you folks do."

Conclusion

To be the people of the name of God means to enjoy the *blessings* of God, including the greatest blessing of all, salvation. It means we are to *worship* God with all our being, to walk in *holiness* as people who are dedicated wholly to Him, and to be a *witness* of Him to the rest of the world. In short, the name is our *identification*.

It is our supreme privilege to be identified with the only saving name, the highest name ever given, the name of Jesus. One day everyone will confess that name (Philippians 2:9-11). Those who confess the name of Jesus now do so in salvation (Romans 10:9-13); those who wait until later will confess that name in judgment.

Let us confess the name of Jesus now in salvation, by repenting in the name of Jesus, being baptized in the name of Jesus, and receiving the Holy Spirit in the name of Jesus (Luke 24:47; Acts 2:38; John 14:26). And from that time forward, let us walk and live in His name, exalting the name of Jesus in our worship, our lifestyle, and our witness.

"And whatsoever ye do in word or deed, do all in the name of the Lord Jesus" (Colossians 3:17).

2

The Significance of God's Name

Parents today usually choose a name for their child because they like the sound of that name or perhaps because they wish to honor someone who bears that name. Often they do not know the original meaning of the name they have chosen.

The Biblical Significance of Names

In Bible days, however, a name was usually chosen for its meaning. The Old Testament records many instances in which the name given to a child related to the circumstances surrounding the child's birth or to the aspirations held by the parents for their child. "In biblical thought a name is not a mere label of identification; it is an expression of the essential nature of its bearer. A man's name reveals his character. . . . The name in the OT is the essence of personality, the expression of innermost being."[1]

God Himself placed great significance upon names. He changed the name of Abram ("exalted father") to Abraham ("father of many") to signify His promise to make him a father of many nations (Genesis 17:5). After Jacob wrestled with God, his name was changed from Jacob ("heel catcher, supplanter") to Israel ("contender with God"). In the New Testament, Simon ("heard") became Peter ("a rock").

God's Character

In a similar manner, God used names and titles to reveal Himself. To Moses God said, "I appeared to Abraham, to Isaac, and to Jacob, as God Almighty, but by My name LORD [Jehovah] I was not known to them. . . . Therefore say to the children of Israel: I am the LORD; I will bring you out from under the burdens of the Egyptians, I will rescue you from their bondage, and I will redeem you with an outstretched arm. . . . Then you shall know that I am the LORD your God, who brings you out from under the burdens of the Egyptians" (Exodus 6:3, 6-7, NKJV).

Abraham used the name Jehovah (Genesis 22:14); however, God did not make known to him the full significance of this name in its redemptive aspect. Abraham saw God's omnipotence as displayed in miracles, but he did not have occasion to see and understand the fullness of God's delivering power. In Exodus 6, God promised to reveal Himself to His people in a new way. He associated His name Jehovah with a new and greater understanding of His character.

To know God's name is to know His true identity, nature, and character. For example, those who know God's name will know that He is faithful and so will trust in Him. "They that know thy name will put their trust in thee: for thou, LORD, hast not forsaken them that seek thee" (Psalm 9:10).

In Exodus 34:5-6, the name represents God's character and glory as revealed to Moses: "And the LORD descended in the cloud, and stood with him there, and proclaimed the name of the LORD. And the LORD passed by before him, and proclaimed, The LORD the LORD God, merciful and gracious, longsuffering, and abundant in goodness and truth." God also told Moses, "The LORD, whose name is Jealous, is a jealous God" (Exodus 34:14). His name signifies that He will not countenance the worship of other gods, who are false.

Throughout the Old Testament, God progressively revealed more about His character to His people, and this progressive revelation was often expressed by new names, such as Jehovah-jireh (Jehovah our Provider) in Genesis 22:14 and Jehovah-rapha (Jehovah our Healer) in Exodus 15:26. People expressed a desire to know more about God by asking to know His name (Genesis 32:29; Judges 13:17; I Kings 8:43).

Pointing to the Incarnation, God promised that one

day His people would know Him plainly, and He expressed this truth by saying, "Therefore my people shall know my name: therefore they shall know in that day that I am he that doth speak: behold, it is I" (Isaiah 52:6). When Jesus reigns over the earth in the Millennium, the truth of God's oneness will be apparent to all, and His essential oneness is represented by His name: "And the LORD shall be king over all the earth: in that day shall there be one LORD, and his name one" (Zechariah 14:9).

God's name is so closely identified with His character that sometimes the Bible uses His name as a synonym for Him. A man was executed under the law for blaspheming "the name," or in other words, "God" (Leviticus 24:11, 15). Many passages in both testaments admonish us to fear, love, bless, praise, and thank God's name, meaning that we are to fear, love, bless, praise, and thank God Himself. (See Deuteronomy 28:58; Psalm 5:11; 54:6; 96:2; Hebrews 6:10; 13:15; Revelation 11:18.)

God's Power

God's name reveals not only His character but also His power. God told Pharaoh through Moses, "And in very deed for this cause have I raised thee up, for to shew in thee my power; and that my name may be declared throughout all the earth" (Exodus 9:16). All nations saw the power of the God of Israel when He defeated the Egyptians, the mightiest kingdom of the day. When people heard the name Jehovah, they thought of Jehovah's omnipotence. Rahab explained to the two Israelite spies, "We have heard how the LORD dried up the water of the Red sea for you, when ye came out of Egypt. . . . And as soon as we had heard these things, our hearts did melt, neither did there remain any more courage in any man, because of you: for the LORD your God, he is God in heaven above, and in earth beneath" (Joshua 2:10-11).

In particular, God's name represents His saving power. Thus David prayed, "Save me, O God, by thy name, and judge me by thy strength" (Psalm 54:1). Salvation is in the name of the LORD (Joel 2:32; Acts 2:21). God will save those who love Him, call upon Him, and know His name (Psalm 91:14).

God's Authority

In addition to power (might, ability), God's name represents His authority (right, warrant). When God promised to send an angel to lead the Israelites, He charged them, "Beware of him, and obey his voice, provoke him not: . . . for my name is in him" (Exodus 23:20-21). The angel (perhaps a manifestation of God) carried divine authority because God invested His name in the angel.

God signifies that people come under His authority by placing His name upon them. (See Deuteronomy 28:10; Amos 9:12.) They are thereby identified with Him, become His possession, and enter into an intimate relationship with Him.

Thus God's people can "call on the name of the

LORD" in petition (I Kings 18:24, 36-37; II Kings 5:11) as well as in worship (Genesis 12:8). By the authority invested in His name, they can expect Him to work miraculously on their behalf.

God's Manifested Presence

The divine name also represents God's immediate presence—His manifested glory, attention, concern, and prayer-answering work. Referring to locations where the Israelites would build an altar of sacrifice, God said, "In all places where I record my name I will come unto thee, and I will bless thee" (Exodus 20:24). God manifested Himself temporarily in these locations. He also promised that He would manifest His presence permanently in the Temple by placing His name there: "But unto the place which the LORD your God shall choose out of all your tribes to put his name there, even unto his habitation shall ye seek, and thither thou shalt come. . . . Then there shall be a place which the LORD your God shall choose to cause his name to dwell there" (Deuteronomy 12:5, 11).

When Solomon prayed at the dedication of the Temple, he acknowledged that the omnipresent God could not be confined to any physical location (I Kings 8:27). Yet he asked for a unique manifestation of God's presence by asking God to place His name in the Temple, as He had promised. Solomon prayed, "That thine eyes may be open toward this house night and day, even toward the place of which thou has said, My name shall be there: that thou mayest hearken unto the prayer which thy servant shall make toward this place" (I Kings 8:29). God answered Solomon's prayer by causing His visible glory to fill the Temple and by placing His name in it (II Chronicles 7:1-2; I Kings 9:3).

Summary

The Interpreter's Dictionary of the Bible explains the significance of God's name in biblical usage:

> The name . . . of God is the key to understanding the biblical doctrine of God. . . . God's self-revelation in history is accompanied by the giving of his personal name, by which his people may worship and address him as "Thou." Thus God's name signifies the personal relation between God and people, which is the supreme characteristic of biblical faith.[2]

> To know the name of God is to know God as he has revealed himself. . . .
> That which is called by Yahweh's name is his possession and therefore comes under both his authority and his protection. . . .
> When used of God, 'name' in the OT has a revelatory content. The name of God means primarily his revealed nature and character—the Savior God as he has manifested himself and desires to be known by man. . . . As expressing essential nature, it [God's name] implies the most complete divine self-disclosure, while the identification of

name and person safeguards the unity of God. . . .

The name of God is frequently used as a synonym for God himself. . . . To know the name of God is to know God himself as he is revealed. . . .

When God acts for his name's sake, he is acting in accordance with his revealed character and to uphold the honor of his revelation. . . .

To call upon the name of God is to invoke him on the basis of his revealed nature and character.[3]

As chapter 1 has shown, the New Testament uses the name of Jesus Christ in the same way that the Old Testament speaks of the name of Jehovah, thereby revealing the identity of Jesus as the one God incarnate. *The Interpreter's Dictionary of the Bible* explains how the doctrine of God's name in the New Testament proclaims the deity of Jesus:

With the name of God there is now linked the name of Jesus Christ, who declares it and so "fulfills" the OT revelation. . . . In him there has been given to men the complete revelation of the divine nature: he has manifested and declared the name of God ([John] 12:28; 17:6, 26). . . .

The distinctive feature of NT usage is the way in which the name of Jesus is either substituted for, or placed alongside, the name of God. Phrases which are used in the OT of the name of God are applied in the NT to the name of Jesus. . . .

The full disclosure of his [God's] nature and

character is given in Jesus Christ, who has manifested his name.[4]

God's name signifies His self-revelation, particularly His character, power, authority, and manifested presence. Jesus is the incarnation of the one true God in all His fullness, and therefore the name of Jesus is the supreme revelation of God today. The fullness of God's character, power, authority, and presence is invested in the name of Jesus and is made available to us when we believe on Jesus and invoke His name.

"For in Him dwells all the fullness of the Godhead bodily; and you are complete in Him, who is the head of all principality and power" (Colossians 2:9-10, NJKV).

3

Call His Name Jesus

And she shall bring forth a son, and thou shalt call his name JESUS: for he shall save his people from their sins (Matthew 1:21).

The Significance of the Name of Jesus

Before the Son of God was born, an angel gave Joseph the name by which He was to be called—Jesus. God chose this name to reveal Himself in flesh as Savior, for the name Jesus literally means "Jehovah-Savior," "Jehovah our Savior," or "Jehovah is Salvation."[1]

Christ fulfilled its meaning as no other man could, for He was God manifested in flesh in order to redeem us. The prophetic message of Isaiah 7:14 said that the name of the Messiah would be called Immanuel, which means "God with us," and the name of Jesus literally fulfills that meaning (Matthew 1:21-23). When we look at the two components of the name Jesus, we find that "Jehovah" corresponds to "God," and "Savior" corresponds to "with us" (for the purpose of salvation).

Jehovah (Yawheh) was the unique, personal name by which the one true God identified Himself to His people in the Old Testament and distinguished Himself from false gods. "I am the LORD [Jehovah]: that is my name" (Isaiah 42:8). In Hebrew, that name is derived from the verb "to be," meaning "He is,"[2] or "He will be." As such, it is the third-person equivalent of the first-person name that God used to reveal Himself to Moses—"I AM" (Exodus 3:14). The connotation of this name—Jehovah or I Am—is the Self-Existing One, the Eternal One, the One who is and who always will be.

By incorporating the supreme Old Testament name Jehovah, the name Jesus encompasses everything the Old Testament reveals about God. In addition, it proclaims the essential truth that the Old Testament God Himself has become our Savior. To see and know Jesus is to see and know God, the Father, in the only way that God can be seen and fully known. Jesus said, "I am the way, the truth, and the life: no man cometh unto the Father, but by me. . . . He that hath seen me hath seen the Father" (John 14:6, 9).

The name of Jesus is the supreme revelation of God's character, for Jesus perfectly manifested the divine nature and attributes, including holiness, righteousness, mercy, truth, love, grace, omniscience, and omnipotence. For example, the Old Testament proclaimed God's love, but only by the revelation of God in Christ do we realize the depths of God's love: "For God so loved the world, that he gave his only begotten Son" (John 3:16). "God commendeth his love toward us, in that, while we were yet sinners, Christ died for us" (Romans 5:8). In Christ, God demonstrated His love in a greater measure than ever before. "Greater love hath no man than this, that a man lay down his life for his friends" (John 15:13).

The name of Jesus is invested with all of God's power and authority. Jesus is "far above all principality, and power, and might, and dominion, and every name that is named, not only in this world, but also in that which is to come" (Ephesians 1:21). Jesus said, "All power is given unto me in heaven and in earth" (Matthew 28:18), and "I am come in my Father's name" (John 5:43).

The miracles of Jesus demonstrated His divine power and authority over nature, disease and sickness, death, the devil and demons, and sin—in short, over every force that can afflict or conquer humanity. "Jesus of Nazareth [was] a man approved of God among you by miracles and wonders and signs, which God did by him in the midst of you" (Acts 2:22).

The teachings of Jesus likewise revealed His divine authority. "The people were astonished at his doctrine: for he taught them as one having authority, and not as the scribes" (Matthew 7:28-29). Even the officers sent to arrest him on one occasion confessed, "No man ever spoke like this Man!" (John 7:46, NKJV).

The works and the words of Jesus were actually the works and words of the Father, who was incarnate in the Son (John 5:17; 8:28; 10:30, 37-38). "Believest thou not that I am in the Father, and the Father in me? the words that I speak unto you I speak not of myself: but the Father that dwelleth in me, he doeth the works" (John 14:10).

The name of Jesus also represents God's very presence. "Where two or three are gathered together in my name, there am I in the midst of them" (Matthew 18:20). In Jesus we have the fullness of God's Spirit. "For in him dwelleth all the fulness of the Godhead bodily. And ye are complete in him" (Colossians 2:9-10).

To know the name of Jesus, then, is to know the supreme revelation of God in human history. For this reason, the apostles understood Christ's command to baptize in the name of the Father, and of the Son, and of the Holy Ghost (that is, in the name of God) to be a reference to the supreme, singular name that reveals God in redemption—the name of Jesus. The Book of Acts records that water baptism was always performed in the name of Jesus Christ.

Consequently, the saints have the name of Jesus invoked over them and are called by His name (Acts 15:17; James 2:7). Not only is this name invoked upon them during the initial act of water baptism, but it remains with them to give power and authority that comes from the presence of Jesus Christ, who abides and actively works in their daily lives. Praying in the name of Jesus expresses faith in His divine character (love, compassion, and desire to help), power (ability to help), authority (right to help), and presence (immediate attention and availability to help).

But the name of Jesus is not a magical formula; prayer is effective only if we have faith in, and truly know, the One whom the name represents (Acts 3:16; 10:43). As the sons of Sceva learned, the devil flees from Jesus and from those who belong to Jesus, but not from those who merely profess Jesus verbally (Acts 19:13-17).

Our Response to the Revelation of the Name

What should our response be to the wonderful revelation of the name of Jesus, a revelation that focuses upon the Incarnation? First, we recognize that salvation and eternal life come through faith in His name (John 20:31). After we repent of our sins, we receive remission of sins at water baptism in the name of Jesus (Luke 24:47; Acts 2:38); and the conversion process is complete when we receive the Holy Spirit through the name of Jesus (John 14:26; Acts 2:38).

Second, we can receive everything we need to live for God through the name of Jesus, including power over Satan, divine healing, and divine protection (Mark 16:17-18). We can pray boldly and confidently in Jesus' name, thereby invoking His character, power, authority, and presence. Jesus promised, "If ye shall ask any thing in my name, I will do it" (John 14:14).

Finally, we are to walk worthy of the name we bear. The apostolic church rejoiced to be counted worthy to suffer for the name of Jesus (Acts 5:40-42). We, too, are willing to endure persecution, opposition, and reproach for His name. We are to live separated, godly lives and proclaim the whole gospel to the whole world.

In everything we say or do, we ask for the Lord's blessing, participation, and assistance. In our speech and conduct, we acknowledge the lordship and deity of Jesus, thereby glorifying the one God who chose to reveal Himself through the name of Jesus. "And whatsoever ye do in word or deed, do all in the name of the Lord Jesus, giving thanks to God and the Father by him" (Colossians 3:17).

4

Yahweh, Yashua, or Jesus?

In recent years a group known as the Assemblies of Yahweh (AY) has placed an unusual emphasis on the spoken pronunciation of the name of God. The AY maintains that God's true name is Yahweh and that salvation comes specifically through this name.

Members of this group also assert that the name of the Son of God must be pronounced as Yashua. Any other form, such as Iesous (Greek) or Jesus (English), is unacceptable. They say that the name Jesus was derived from the names of the Greek gods Zeus and Dionysus, because the last two letters of each name are identical. One of their writers has even alleged that the name Jesus means "the pig," because *Je* supposedly means "the" and *sus* supposedly means "pig."

Scholars generally agree that the original Hebrew pronunciation of the Old Testament name of God was Yahweh or something similar; certainly the pronunciation Jehovah is a later English construction. Most scholars also agree that in New Testament times the Hebrew or Aramaic pronunciation of the name Jesus was Yeshua or Y'shua (not Yashua) and that this name is identical to the Old Testament name Joshua. Let us analyze the position of the AY, then, in the light of Scripture.

First, the AY does not attribute full deity to Jesus Christ as the Bible does, but it speaks of God and Jesus as if they were two separate persons. Its view of Jesus is similar to that of Jehovah's Witnesses; both use the designation C.E. (Common Era) instead of A.D. (Anno Domini = in the year of the Lord), apparently because they do not want to acknowledge Jesus as the supreme Lord. The AY exalts Yahweh as the highest name of God, not realizing that the New Testament provides us with a greater revelation of God and His name. Yahweh of the Old Testament manifested Himself in flesh to be our Savior in the New Testament. The name Jesus incorporates the revelation of God contained in both testaments, for it literally means "Yahweh-Savior" or "Yahweh is salvation."

Although others have borne the name Joshua, Yeshua, or Jesus, Jesus Christ of Nazareth alone truly personifies the meaning of that name. He is "God with us" (Matthew 1:23), who came to "save his people from their sins" (Matthew 1:21), and "in him dwelleth all the fulness of the Godhead bodily" (Colossians 2:9). Consequently, the name of Jesus is the only saving name, the highest name ever known to humanity, the name at which every knee shall bow, the name that every tongue shall confess, and the name in which we are to say and do all things (Acts 4:12; Ephesians 1:20-21; Philippians 2:9-11; Colossians 3:17). For this reason, the early church baptized in the name of Jesus, not in the name of Yahweh (Acts 2:38).

Second, the AY wrongly attaches saving efficacy to the pronunciation of God's name in a certain way—to the vibrations of sound waves. In actuality, the significance of the name rests in its meaning. It is effective because of the One it represents, and it is effective only when we have faith in the One it represents. When we call the name of Jesus in faith, He responds to our cry and performs a work in our lives.

This is what the Bible means when it says we receive healing and salvation through the name of Jesus: "And his name through faith in his name hath made this man strong" (Acts 3:16). "Through his name whosoever believeth in him shall receive remission of sins" (Acts 10:43). Answers to prayer did not come to the early church because of a certain pronunciation of the name, but because they invoked the name in faith.

The seven sons of Sceva attempted to cast out demons by calling on the same name that Paul used with success. They could not cast the demons out because, unlike Paul, they did not have a personal relationship with Jesus Christ (Acts 19:13-17). Their problem was not faulty pronunciation but deficient faith.

A study of human language and speech shows that it is a mistake to attach saving efficacy to a certain pronunciation of the name. No one pronounces words exactly alike; voice prints are as unique as fingerprints. Even if we could be certain of the original spelling of the Old Testament name of God, no one can know the exact pronunciation that the ancient Hebrews attached to the individual vowels and consonants. Moreover, ancient Hebrew had different dialects, and in one of them there was no *sh* sound in certain cases (Judges 12:4-6).

If salvation depends upon exact pronunciation, what happens to people with speech impediments, accents, or dialects? What happens to people whose languages do not contain certain sounds? For example, Greek does not have a *sh* sound, and Korean does not have a final *s* sound.

Third, the position of the AY would require us to reject the New Testament that we now have, including all known manuscripts and versions. The Greek New Testament, including all ancient Greek manuscripts in existence, uses the name Iesous. The AY has to maintain that it was not written by the apostles or the early church, for if they used Iesous in even one passage, then the AY position is disproved.

While a few scholars believe that Matthew was originally written in Hebrew or Aramaic, it is impossible to maintain that the entire New Testament was so written. The Gospel of Luke and the Book of Acts were written by a Gentile, Luke, to another Gentile, Theophilus, and it is unlikely that either of them knew Hebrew or Aramaic. Paul wrote his letters to Gentile churches. Clearly, these writers used Greek. Moreover, a study of New Testament style, grammar, idioms, and vocabulary demonstrates that Greek was the original language.

For the AY position to be correct, Jesus, the apostles, and the early church would have had to use the early Hebrew name Yashua and never any other variation, even when speaking or writing in the Hebrew, Aramaic, or Greek of their day. We do not have a single manuscript or ancient version of the New Testament that does so, and no one has ever recorded the existence of such a manuscript. No scholar has ever produced evidence that there was such a manuscript.

Fourth, the scholarship of the AY is faulty. *Webster's Unabridged Dictionary* clearly shows that the English name Jesus came from the Latin Iesus, from the Greek Iesous, from the Hebrew Yeshua. Yeshua, in turn, is a contraction of the original Hebrew name Yehoshua. This long form occurs in Numbers 13:16, and it comes from *Yah* (a short form of Yahweh) and *hoshia* (meaning "to help," with the later connotation "to save").

To be consistent the AY should not use the contracted form Yashua, but the original form Yehoshua or perhaps even Yahweh-hoshia. Moreover, the formation of the English name Jesus was not due to any sinister motive or meaning; it occurred according to standard rules and developments in Hebrew, Greek, Latin, and English.

It is not accurate to say that the name Jesus came from the combination of two separate words *Je* and *sus,* supposedly meaning "the pig," any more than my name David comes from *Da* and *vid,* with the meaning of "daytime video." Moreover, no dictionary says that *je* means "the" or that *sus* means "pig."

The relation of the endings of Dionysus, Zeus, and Jesus is purely coincidental. In the original Greek there is no connection, for the endings are, respectively, *-os, -eus,* and *-ous.* (Both *eu* and *ou* are diphthongs, which means that the vowels are to be pronounced as one unit and not to be regarded as separate sounds or syllables.)

Fifth, as a practical matter, God Himself honors the use of the English name Jesus. When people pray by using this name in faith, they receive the Holy Spirit, answers to prayer, healing, and deliverance from demons.

In conclusion, the name of Jesus may be pronounced in many different ways in various languages, dialects, and accents. In all of its forms, it means the same thing: the one true God of the Old Testament has become our Savior in the historical person of Jesus of Nazareth. When a person uses the name with that understanding, and with faith in Jesus as Lord and Messiah, then regardless of the language he speaks, his prayer will reach the throne of God and his invocation of God's name will be effective.

5

Baptism in the Name of Jesus

Every time the Bible records the name or formula associated with an actual baptism in the New Testament church, it describes the name Jesus. All five such accounts occur in the Book of Acts, the history book of the early church. Let us examine each one.

The Jews on the Day of Pentecost

On the birthday of the New Testament church, the first Day of Pentecost after the ascension of Jesus, the Holy Spirit baptized the waiting 120 disciples, just as Jesus had promised. (See Acts 2.) When they were filled with the Spirit, they began to speak miraculously in languages they had never learned, as the Spirit gave the utterance, and this miracle attracted a large multitude. The apostle Peter, with the support of the other eleven apostles, preached the gospel to the thousands of curious onlookers (Acts 2:14). The crowd consisted of Jews from various nations who had gathered in Jerusalem to celebrate the Feast of Pentecost.

Peter began by explaining what had aroused their curiosity—the phenomenon of speaking in tongues—and identified it with the prophecy of Joel that God would pour out His Spirit in the last days. Peter continued quoting from Joel until he reached the following statement: "Whosoever shall call on the name of the Lord shall be saved" (Acts 2:21). From this point he introduced the crowd to the Lord—Jesus Christ of Nazareth. He preached the simple gospel message, namely, the death, burial, and resurrection of Jesus Christ (Acts 2:22-36; I Corinthians 15:1-4). His message culminated with the proclamation, "God hath made that same Jesus, whom ye have crucified, both Lord and Christ" (Acts 2:36).

Conviction of sin gripped the hearts of the listeners, and they "said unto Peter and to the rest of the apostles, Men and brethren, what shall we do?" (Acts 2:37). They were not asking how to receive an extra blessing, but how to obey the gospel Peter had just preached. They wanted to know how to be forgiven of their sins, including their rejection of the Messiah. They wanted to know how to accept Jesus as Lord and Messiah. In short, they wanted to know how to be saved.

Peter and the other apostles told them how to respond to the gospel message: "Repent, and be baptized every one of you in the name of Jesus Christ for the remission of sins, and ye shall receive the gift of the Holy Ghost. For the promise is unto you, and to your children, and to all that are afar off, even as many as the Lord our God shall call" (Acts 2:38-39). About three thousand people believed and obeyed these instructions and were baptized accordingly (Acts 2:41).

By repentance people die to sin and self-will, thereby identifying with Christ's death. By baptism they are buried with Christ. And by receiving the Holy Spirit, the Spirit of the risen Lord, they identify with Christ's resurrection. (See Romans 6:1-7; 7:6; 8:2, 10-11.)

For our study, it is important to note that the apostles commanded "every one of you" to be baptized in the name of Jesus Christ and that the message applied to "as many as the Lord our God shall call." Baptism in Jesus' name is an integral part of responding properly to the gospel message and accepting Jesus as Lord.

Despite this clear, unambiguous instruction and the universality of its application, some people argue that it is directed only to Jews. Since the Jews already acknowledge the Father, they contend, the Jews merely need to add a profession of faith in Jesus, but the rest of humanity should be baptized into a trinity of divine persons. The account in Acts 8 refutes this theory, however.

The Samaritans

In Acts 8, Philip the evangelist brought the gospel to the Samaritans, who were descendants of intermarriages between Jews and Gentiles. Although they were not Jews, they also "were baptized in the name of the Lord Jesus" (Acts 8:16).

Some people try to explain that even though the Samaritans were not Jews, their religion was largely based upon Judaism and like the Jews they already acknowledged the Father. Thus, these people claim, baptism in the name of Jesus alone was appropriate for them as well but is not meant for everyone. The next account, however, dispels this supposition.

The Gentiles

In Acts 10, God led the apostle Peter to preach the gospel to the Gentiles. As he preached to Cornelius, a Roman centurion, and his household, the Holy Spirit fell upon them, just as on the Day of Pentecost. The Jewish Christians who had accompanied Peter were astonished "because that on the Gentiles also was poured out the gift of the Holy Ghost" (Acts 10:45).

From this reaction, it is obvious that these people were Gentiles and were not previous converts to Judaism (proselytes). Gentile proselytes were considered full Jews, and proselytes had been in the crowd on the Day of Pentecost (Acts 2:10). But these people were uncircumcised Gentiles, and consequently Peter later had to explain to the church why he had broken Jewish tradition by visiting the home of unconverted Gentiles and eating with them (Acts 11:1-4).

Although these Gentiles were neither Jews nor Samaritans, immediately after they received the Holy Spirit, Peter "commanded them to be baptized in the name of the Lord" (Acts 10:48). Of course, the name of the Lord is Jesus (Philippians 2:11). In fact, the oldest Greek manuscripts in existence today actually read "in the name of Jesus Christ" here, as do most versions today.

Some try to explain that Jesus Name baptism is only for Gentiles who already believe in the God of Israel, but I Corinthians shows that it is also for the most pagan of Gentiles. Corinth was a Greek city notorious for idolatry and immorality. The church in Corinth was full of divisions, with various groups claiming to be followers of Paul, Apollos, Peter, or Christ (I Corinthians 1:12). When Paul rebuked them for their divisions, he asked, "Is Christ divided? was Paul crucified for you? or were ye baptized in the name of Paul" (I Corinthians 1:13). The obvious answer to the two latter questions is, "No, Jesus Christ was crucified for us. No, we were baptized in the name of Jesus Christ." Since they were baptized in the name of Jesus Christ, not Paul, they belonged to Christ, not Paul. Paul's point was this: Since Jesus died for the whole church and the whole church was baptized in His name, the whole church should unite in following Him. If the Corinthians were not baptized in Jesus' name, Paul's argument makes no sense.

A few chapters later, Paul alluded to their Jesus

Name baptism again, showing it was administered to everyone, even those who had been the most pagan and immoral: "Be not deceived: neither fornicators, nor idolaters, nor adulterers, nor effeminate, nor abusers of themselves with mankind, nor thieves, nor covetous, nor drunkards, nor revilers, nor extortioners, shall inherit the kingdom of God. And such were some of you: but ye are washed, but ye are sanctified, but ye are justified in the name of the Lord Jesus, and by the Spirit of our God" (I Corinthians 6:9-11).

In short, the New Testament reveals that people in every conceivable class are to be baptized in the name of Jesus—whether Jews, Samaritans (part Jews), or Gentiles (non Jews).

The Disciples of John at Ephesus

Faced with the undeniable evidence we have discussed, many people concede that baptism in the name of Jesus is acceptable. Some even agree that it is the original method and that it is to be preferred. Yet many of the same people say, "I have already been baptized another way, so I don't see the need to be rebaptized. After all, it's the intent of my heart that counts." While this reasoning may seem plausible to the human mind, let us see how the Bible addresses this issue.

In Acts 19, Paul met some disciples at Ephesus who had been baptized according to the teaching of John the Baptist. John was a prophet of God, and his baptism was ordained of God for his time (Luke 7:28-30). John baptized by immersion in water (Matthew 3:16;

John 3:23), and he required repentance and confession of sins before he would administer baptism (Mark 1:4-5; Luke 3:7-8).

Nevertheless, when Paul learned that these disciples at Ephesus had received only John's baptism, he explained to them that John's ministry pointed to Jesus Christ, and then he baptized them a second time. This time, "they were baptized in the name of the Lord Jesus" (Acts 19:5). The only difference between the two baptisms was their new understanding of Jesus and the invocation of the name of Jesus upon them.

Although their prior baptism had been a positive step towards God, Paul did not tell these men to be content with it. Nor did he say that their new knowledge and faith made a further step unnecessary. Instead, he considered the name of Jesus to be so important that, although their previous baptism was done upon repentance and faith, by immersion in water, and by a man of God, he rebaptized them in order for them to take on the name of Jesus in baptism.

Likewise, we do not attack, ridicule, or condemn anyone who has taken a step towards God in baptism. In a world of unbelief, apathy, and even hatred of God, any attempt to please God and fulfill His Word is commendable. But once a person understands the complete biblical message of the identity of Jesus Christ and the importance of baptism in the name of Jesus Christ, he should not be content with what he has done in the past. If he has never been baptized in the name of Jesus, following the apostolic precedent he should be rebaptized with the invocation of that name.

The Apostle Paul

Some people try to sidestep the whole issue of the baptismal formula by saying that "in the name of Jesus" does not mean to invoke the name but merely to act upon the power and authority of Jesus. But the way to act upon His power and authority is to invoke His name in faith in obedience to His Word.

The conversion of Saul of Tarsus (later the apostle Paul) provides a good example. When Saul came to Ananias as the Lord had directed him, Ananias instructed him, "Arise, and be baptized, and wash away thy sins, calling on the name of the Lord" (Acts 22:16). Saul knew exactly what the Lord's name was, for he had recently asked, "Who art thou, Lord?" and the Lord had replied, "I am Jesus" (Acts 9:5).

The command of Ananias shows that the name of Jesus is to be called at water baptism. The Greek verb translated "calling" here literally means "invoking." (For further discussion of this point, see chapter 7.)

The Significance of the Name in Baptism

The Book of Acts establishes that the apostles and the early church consistently baptized in the name of Jesus Christ. This pattern is the norm for the church today. It is our responsibility to obey the commands and examples in the Book of Acts regardless of whether we understand the reasons for this practice or the importance of it. Obedience is the only course open to us if we truly accept the Bible as our sole authority for faith and practice and if we truly desire to make Jesus the Lord of all of our life, including our thoughts, values, beliefs, and practices.

Baptism in the name of Jesus Christ is not an arbitrary practice, however. Using the name of Jesus in baptism is inextricably linked with the very purpose of baptism itself. All the reasons for being baptized in water are also reasons for invoking the name of Jesus at baptism. If someone wishes to be baptized but refuses the invocation of the name of Jesus, he has not fully grasped the reasons why he should be baptized. Let us examine these reasons.

1. As a minimum, all groups in Christendom agree that the purpose of water baptism is *to express faith in Jesus as Lord and Savior.* When the listeners on the Day of Pentecost accepted Jesus as Lord and Messiah, they were baptized (Acts 2:36-38, 41). When the Samaritans "believed Philip preaching . . . concerning the kingdom of God, and the name of Jesus Christ, they were baptized" (Acts 8:12). When the disciples of John at Ephesus heard that Jesus was the fulfillment of the prophecy of John the Baptist, they were baptized (Acts 19:4-5). When the Corinthians "believed on the Lord," they were baptized (Acts 18:8). The proper way to express faith in Jesus is to confess His name, and in each of the cases just cited, the candidates expressed their faith in Jesus by being baptized in the name of Jesus.

2. Baptism is *"for the remission of sins"* (Acts 2:38), or to "wash away . . . sins" (Acts 22:16), and the name

of Jesus is the only name given for remission of sins. "Through his name whosoever believeth in him shall receive remission of sins" (Acts 10:43). Thus the proper way to seek remission of sins at baptism is to invoke the name of Jesus in faith. Acts 2:38 and Acts 22:16 not only connect remission of sins with water baptism, but they specifically connect remission of sins with water baptism in the name of Jesus.

3. Baptism is *part of our salvation* (Mark 16:16; I Peter 3:21), and the name of Jesus is the only name given for salvation. "Neither is there salvation in any other: for there is none other name under heaven given among men, whereby we must be saved" (Acts 4:12). (See also Acts 2:21; Romans 10:9, 13.) Thus the proper way to integrate water baptism with the New Testament salvation experience is to invoke the name of Jesus.

4. Baptism is *a burial with Jesus Christ* (Romans 6:4; Colossians 2:12). The Spirit of God did not die for us; only Jesus the man died for us and was buried in the tomb. To be buried with Jesus Christ, we should be baptized in His name.

5. Baptism is *part of our personal identification with Jesus Christ.* "So many of us as were baptized into Jesus Christ were baptized into his death" (Romans 6:3). "For as many of you as have been baptized into Christ have put on Christ" (Galatians 3:27). If we seek to be identified with Him, we should take on His name.

6. Baptism is *part of the new birth* by which we are born into the spiritual family of God (John 3:5; Titus

3:5). We can also view the conversion experience, of which baptism is a part, as an adoption into the spiritual family of God (Romans 8:15-16). A newly born or adopted child always takes on the name of his new family. Since we seek to enter into the church of Jesus Christ, which is called His body and His bride, we should take on His name. (See Ephesians 5:23, 29-32.)

7. Baptism is *part of our spiritual circumcision,* or initiation into the new covenant (Colossians 2:11-13). Under the old covenant a male child officially received his name at his physical circumcision. (See Luke 2:21.) Water baptism is the time when our new family name is invoked upon us at our spiritual circumcision.

In connection with the last two points, we know that the identifying name of our new spiritual family is Jesus, for at least two reasons. First, it is the only name in which we can receive salvation. (See John 14:6; Acts 4:12.) Second, it is the supreme name by which God has chosen to reveal Himself to us. "Wherefore God also hath highly exalted him, and given him a name which is above every name: that at the name of Jesus every knee should bow, of things in heaven, and things in earth, and things under the earth; and that every tongue should confess that Jesus Christ is Lord, to the glory of God the Father" (Philippians 2:9-11).

Some people say that the supreme name described in Philippians 2:9 is Lord. That is, God has given the man Jesus the supreme title of Lord. Although Jesus was openly and miraculously declared to be Lord by the resurrection and ascension, this declaration does not detract from the supremacy of Jesus as the personal name of God incarnate. The title of Lord serves to magnify the name of Jesus and underscore its true meaning.

As an analogy, the highest political office and title in the United States is that of president. When Abraham Lincoln was the president he had the highest title; nevertheless, his unique name—the name that embodied his legal identity, power, and authority—was still Abraham Lincoln. He could not merely sign documents as "Mr. President"; he had to sign them as "Abraham Lincoln" in order for his signature to be effective.

Philippians 2:10 specifically states that at the name of Jesus every knee will bow. Verses 10-11 do not merely say that everyone will acknowledge the existence of a supreme Lord, for many unsaved people already do that; the significance is that everyone will acknowledge that *Jesus* is the one Lord. As Bauer's lexicon translates, "when the name of Jesus is mentioned" every knee will bow and every tongue will confess that Jesus Christ is Lord.[1] And this event will fulfill the proclamation of Jehovah, who said, "Unto me every knee shall bow, every tongue shall swear" (Isaiah 45:23). At the last judgment, every being will acknowledge Jesus as the one God incarnate.

Colossians 3:17 says, "Whatsoever ye do in word or deed, do all in the name of the Lord Jesus, giving thanks to God and the Father by him." This verse does not require us to pronounce the name of Jesus orally before every activity, but it deals with the attitude in which we conduct every activity. All our words and actions should be consistent with the invocation of Jesus as Lord. When there is cause to invoke God's name formally, such as at water baptism, which is both word and deed, this verse applies in a specific way, telling us to approach God in the name of the Lord Jesus. Just as we pray, lay hands on the sick, and cast out demons in the name of Jesus, so we should baptize in the name of Jesus.

Conclusion

Using the name of Jesus in the baptismal formula expresses faith in

- the *person of Christ* (who He really is);
- the *work of Christ* (His death, burial, and resurrection for our salvation); and
- the *power and authority of Christ* (His ability to save us by Himself).

In short, baptism in the name of Jesus signifies that we trust in Jesus alone as our Savior, and thus it expresses the essence of saving faith. Since the only one who can take away sins is Jesus—not us by our deeds, not the water, and not the preacher—we call upon Him in faith, depending on Him to do the work.

The Bible teaches that everyone should be baptized in the name of Jesus Christ, and it reveals that every reason for baptism is specifically a reason for baptism in the name of Jesus. Thus baptism in the name of Jesus demonstrates reverence for and obedience to the Word of God over and above human tradition, convenience, or peer pressure.

In view of the scriptural significance of the name of Jesus, why would anyone refuse to be baptized in Jesus' name? Why would anyone hesitate to take on the name of the One who died for us and to identify publicly with Him? Why would anyone reject the only saving name, the name that is above every name?

6

The Baptismal Formula according to Matthew 28:19

As the Book of Acts and the Epistles clearly teach, the early church baptized in the name of Jesus Christ and thereby established the pattern for us to follow. Only one verse in the Bible could possibly allude to any other baptismal formula—Matthew 28:19—so let us examine its teaching in context.

And Jesus came and spake unto them, saying, All power is given unto me in heaven and in earth. Go ye therefore, and teach all nations, baptizing them in the name of the Father, and of the Son, and of the Holy Ghost: teaching them to observe all things whatsoever I have commanded you: and, lo, I am with you alway, even unto the end of the world (Matthew 28:18-20).

General Considerations for Interpreting Matthew 28:19

Matthew 28:19 speaks of baptism "in the name of the Father, and of the Son, and of the Holy Ghost," while Acts and the Epistles speak of baptism "in the name of Jesus Christ." Before analyzing Matthew 28:19 in detail, let us consider the possible explanations as to why these two different phrases appear in Scripture.

First, one could say that the two phrases are contradictory and we must choose one over the other. This explanation violates two basic principles of biblical interpretation: (1) the inspiration of Scripture and (2) the unity of Scripture. Since the Bible is the inspired, infallible, inerrant Word of God, it does not contain error. Since the Bible is God's Word to humanity, it presents a unified message and does not contradict itself.

Some people use a form of this argument by saying, "I would rather obey the words of Jesus (in Matthew) than the words of Peter (in Acts)." But this statement assumes that Scripture contradicts itself and that the apostles were in error. If this were the case, we would not be able to trust the Bible at all. If we cannot trust the apostles, it would be futile to appeal to the words of Jesus, for Jesus did not write any books of the Bible. We must trust Matthew's record of what Jesus said just as we must trust Luke's record in Acts and Paul's statements in his epistles.

Second, one could say that neither phrase describes the baptismal formula. If so, we have no biblical formula for water baptism. This is very unlikely in light of the importance of baptism, the need to distinguish Christian baptism from other types of baptism, the common-sense reading of the passages in question, and the universal Christian practice from the most ancient times of using a baptismal formula. Clearly, some sort of formula is necessary to identify baptism as baptism and to express its significance.

This explanation makes the baptismal formula an irrelevant technicality. By similar reasoning, one could justify celebrating the Lord's Supper with cake and punch, performing baptism by sprinkling with milk, or even omitting the baptismal ceremony altogether. If the formula is irrelevant, baptism in any name or no name would be valid Christian baptism, which is absurd. Obviously, the spiritual significance of baptism is expressed by the formula used and the name invoked.

Third, one could say that the two phrases describe two completely different formulas, either of which is acceptable. This explanation faces some of the same problems as the preceding two, for it seems to make the Bible contradict itself and minimizes the significance of the baptismal formula. It indicates that there can be conflicting methods of Christian initiation. But there is only one God and one message of salvation for all people (Romans 3:29-30). In particular, there is only one Christian baptism (Ephesians 4:5).

In the final analysis, this explanation proves too much, for if Matthew and Acts present two different formulas, there is no evidence that the early church used both. Rather, it would appear that Jesus gave one formula but the early church consistently used another one, thereby disobeying the Lord from the start. Clearly, this conclusion is untenable.

Fourth, one could say that both phrases describe the same baptismal formula. This view preserves the inspiration, inerrancy, and unity of Scripture. It also rests upon two other important principles of biblical interpretation: (1) Scripture interprets Scripture and (2) truth has several witnesses. (See II Corinthians 13:1.) The former principle tells us that the best interpreter of a passage of Scripture is the rest of Scripture. The latter principle tells us that the truth, especially important points of doctrine and practice, can be established in several ways, not just by one isolated text. While every verse of Scripture is inspired of God and therefore authoritative, if someone builds a doctrine on one verse alone and cannot provide additional support in Scripture, it is likely that he is misinterpreting or misapplying that one verse.

This harmonizing explanation suggests that we should start with the historical accounts in the Book of Acts and interpret Matthew 28:19 in light of them, rather than vice versa. In a situation where there are many witnesses, all of whom are trustworthy, we should rely foremost on the many witnesses that use similar language and then harmonize a lone witness that explains the matter from a somewhat different perspective.

In connection with this point, we should note that the apostle Matthew recorded Matthew 28:19 and also stood with Peter when he preached on the Day of Pentecost (Acts 2:14). The question, "Men and brethren, what shall we do?" was addressed to all the apostles (Acts 2:37). If Peter had given an incorrect answer when he told the crowd to be baptized in the name of Jesus Christ (Acts 2:38), Matthew would have corrected him. Peter heard Jesus speak Matthew 28:19, Matthew heard Peter speak Acts 2:38, and only about one or two weeks separated the two events. Clearly, both apostles understood that the two statements harmonized.

Moreover, we must realize that the Gospel of Matthew was not written until long after the occurrence of the events recorded in Acts. Most scholars say Matthew was written about A.D. 62-63 or later. As the accounts in Acts show, prospective converts heard the preaching of the apostles concerning baptism in the name of Jesus before they heard oral traditions about the words of Jesus in Matthew 28:19. And the early church practiced baptism in the name of Jesus on the authority of the apostles long before they were able to read the words of Jesus as recorded in Matthew. In actual life, then, the church interpreted the words of Matthew 28:19 in light of their new-birth experience and historical practice, not vice versa. When the Gospel of Matthew was distributed, there is no evidence that the church changed its baptismal practice; instead they

In the Name of Jesus

evidently understood Matthew 28:19 to be consistent with their existing practice.

Analysis of the Text of Matthew 28:19

Leaving the foregoing considerations aside, let us examine Matthew 28:19 itself to see what the verse teaches. In studying a particular passage of Scripture, we should use the grammatical-historical method, sometimes called the literal method. That is, we should seek to understand the words according to their ordinary and apparent meaning, according to their historical and grammatical usage. In making this determination, several factors are important, including biblical history, biblical geography, biblical culture, setting (immediate background or situation), literary mold (genre), special literary forms (such as figures of speech and parables), context (immediate literary passage), word meanings, grammar (syntax), and the harmony of Scripture. Five of these factors are particularly relevant to our inquiry concerning Matthew 28:19.

Grammar

Matthew 28:19 describes only one name, for *name* is singular and not plural. (If someone thinks it is inappropriate to emphasize this distinction, he should read Galatians 3:16, where Paul placed utmost importance on the singular in Genesis 12:7; 22:17-18.) Many commentators have recognized that the singular form is significant here. For example, Matthew Henry wrote, "We are baptized not into the 'names' but into the name, of the Father, Son, and Spirit, which plainly intimates that these are one, and their name one."[1] This understanding accords with Old Testament predictions that God would be revealed and known by one name: "Therefore my people shall know my name" (Isaiah 52:6). "In that day shall there be one LORD, and his name one" (Zechariah 14:9).

Under any interpretation, the titles of Father, Son, and Holy Ghost describe the one God. What, then, is the one supreme name by which God is revealed today? Some commentators say it is Jehovah, but as chapters 1-4 have shown, the Old Testament name Jehovah has been incorporated into and superseded by the New Testament name Jesus.

Father, Son, and Holy Ghost are not proper names but descriptive titles. Even if they were proper names, this verse specifically describes only one name, not three. We must still ask what is the one proper name of the Father, Son, and Holy Ghost.

Without doubt the name of the Son is Jesus, for the angel told Joseph, "And she shall bring forth a son, and thou shalt call his name JESUS" (Matthew 1:21).

Jesus said, "I am come in my Father's name" (John 5:43). He said to the Father, "I have manifested thy name . . . I have declared unto them thy name" (John 17:6, 26). The Old Testament predicted that the Messiah would declare God's name (Psalm 22:22; Hebrews 2:12). Jesus received His name by inheritance (Hebrews 1:4). The name that Jesus actually received, came in, manifested, and declared was Jesus. When He performed miracles, it was the name of Jesus that was broadcast from person to person and village to village. In short, the Father has revealed Himself to the world by the name of Jesus.

Jesus also said, "But the Comforter, which is the Holy Ghost, whom the Father will send in my name, he shall teach you all things" (John 14:26). People receive the Holy Spirit by turning away from sin and turning to Jesus in faith. In short, they receive the Holy Spirit in the name of Jesus.

Word Study

A study of the biblical use of the titles of Father, Son, and Holy Ghost underscores the interpretation just given. The Bible teaches emphatically that God is absolutely one (Deuteronomy 6:4; Isaiah 44:6-8, 24; Galatians 3:20), so these titles cannot refer to separate personalities or distinct centers of consciousness in God.

The title of Father refers to God in parental relationship to humanity. The one God is the Father of all humans and all spirits by creation (Malachi 2:10; Hebrews 12:9). In a special way, He is the Father of His chosen people, who have been adopted into His spiritual family (Deuteronomy 32:6; Romans 8:15). And He is uniquely the Father of the only begotten Son of God, for the Spirit of God—not any man—actually caused the baby to be conceived in the womb of the virgin Mary (Matthew 1:18, 20).

The title of Holy Ghost, or Holy Spirit, refers to

the one God in His spiritual essence and action. God is the Holy One (Isaiah 54:5), the only one who is holy in and of Himself. Other holy beings are simply partakers of His holiness (Hebrews 12:10). And God is Spirit (John 4:24). Holiness forms the basis of his moral attributes, while spirituality forms the basis of his nonmoral attributes. The title of Holy Spirit, then, simply describes who and what God is. The Bible uses it particularly in reference to God's activity in the world and in human lives, performing works that only a Spirit can do. (See Genesis 1:2; John 3:5; Acts 1:8; 2:1-4.) The one God, the Father, is actually the Holy Spirit. (See Matthew 1:18, 20 with Luke 2:49; Matthew 10:20; Romans 8:15-16; I Peter 1:2 with Jude 1.)

The title of Son relates to the Incarnation, to God manifested in the flesh. As a human, Jesus was called the Son of God because the Spirit of God literally caused Him to be conceived miraculously (Luke 1:35). The Son was begotten on a certain day (Hebrews 1:5). The Son was made of a woman and sent out into the world on a divine mission (Galatians 4:4). The Son died (Romans 5:10). These examples show that the title of Son never refers to deity alone, but always to God as revealed in humanity or to the humanity in which God was revealed. The deity indwelling the Son is actually the Father. (See John 10:30, 38; 14:9-11.)

When we understand the biblical definitions of these titles, we readily see that Matthew 28:19 does not speak of three different names that identify three different persons. Rather, it uses three titles of the one

God. These three titles do not describe eternal divisions in God's nature; rather, they focus on three roles God assumed for our redemption. In order to provide the sinless, substitutionary, atoning sacrifice for our sin, God came in flesh in the Son. In begetting the Son and establishing a relationship to humanity, God is the Father. In regenerating and transforming those who believe and obey the gospel, God is the Holy Spirit. Our salvation experience, which includes water baptism, depends upon each of these aspects of God's redemptive work. Jesus is the one name that encompasses these three roles, for it is the one name given for our salvation (Acts 4:12).

For further discussion of these titles and the nature of God, see David Bernard, *The Oneness of God* (Hazelwood, MO: Word Aflame Press, 1983).

Setting

To interpret a scriptural passage, it is important to ascertain its setting or background. Instead of approaching Matthew 28:19 with nineteen hundred years of doctrinal development and attaching modern theological meanings to its words, we should try to understand the verse from the point of view of the original speaker, audience, occasion, and purpose.

Jesus spoke the words of Matthew 28:19 to His disciples, who were devout Jews trained from birth to believe that God is absolutely one (Deuteronomy 6:4-9). He commended this view (Mark 12:28-31; John 4:22) and said nothing to modify it in any way. The terminology and concepts of trinitarianism did not appear until about A.D. 200, so the disciples did not think in those categories. There was no chance of Jesus' words being interpreted in a trinitarian way at the time.

The disciples had long confessed Jesus as the Son of God (Matthew 16:16), and just a few weeks earlier, Jesus had removed any uncertainty or misunderstanding from their minds as to His true identity. Just before His crucifixion, He told them that He was the Father incarnate. When Philip asked to see the Father, Jesus replied, "Have I been so long time with you, and yet hast thou not known me, Philip? he that hath seen me hath seen the Father; and how sayest thou then, Shew us the Father? Believest thou not that I am in the Father, and the Father in me? the words that I speak unto you I speak not of myself: but the Father that dwelleth in me, he doeth the works" (John 14:9-10). He explained that the only way they could ever see the Father, who is an invisible Spirit, was to see Him, for He was the revelation of the Father in flesh.

On the same occasion, He explained the identity of the Holy Spirit. "And I will pray the Father, and he shall give you another Comforter, that he may abide with you for ever; even the Spirit of truth; whom the world cannot receive, because it seeth him not, neither knoweth him: but ye know him; for he dwelleth with you, and shall be in you. I will not leave you comfortless: I will come to you" (John 14:16-18). The Spirit they would soon receive was really not another person; rather, the Spirit would be Jesus in another form. He

In the Name of Jesus

dwelt with them in flesh, but soon He would come back to dwell in them spiritually.

After the Resurrection, Thomas confessed Jesus as "my Lord and my God" in front of all the apostles, and Jesus commended him for his faith (John 20:28-29).

When Jesus gave the instructions of Matthew 28:19 to His disciples, these lessons were fresh in their minds. They clearly understood that Jesus was the one God of the Old Testament, the one God of their historic faith, revealed in flesh. As to His deity He was the Father, as to His humanity He was the Son, and He would soon come back to dwell in them as the Holy Spirit. It was easy for them to understand that the name of the Father, Son, and Holy Ghost is Jesus.

Context

In verse 18 Jesus said, "All power is given unto me in heaven and in earth." Verse 19 continues, "Go ye therefore. . . . " Jesus did not mean, "I have all power; therefore, baptize in three different names (or in another name), and I will be with you always." Rather, He was saying, "I have all power, so baptize in my name, and I will be with you always." G. R. Beasley-Murray, a Baptist scholar, has explained, "A whole group of exegetes and critics have recognized that the opening declaration of Mt. 28:18 demands a Christological statement to follow it: 'All authority in heaven and on earth has been given to Me' leads us to expect as a consequence, 'Go and make disciples *unto Me* among all the nations, baptizing them in *My* name, teaching them to observe all *I* commanded you.' "[2]

Because of the context, many scholars think that verse 19 originally contained a Jesus Name formula that was changed by postapostolic Christianity.[3] They note that the church historian Eusebius, who lived in the 300s, often quoted verse 19 by using the phrase "in my name."[4] He did this many times before the Council of Nicea but never afterwards. Others hold that verse 19 describes the nature of baptism and was not originally interpreted as a baptismal formula.[5]

The second position seems likely. The problem with the textual argument is that all existing manuscripts contain the present wording of Matthew 28:19. While many scholars see that the context demands a Jesus Name formula, due to their trinitarian preconceptions they fail to see that the existing wording does in fact describe baptism in the name of Jesus. The evidence from Eusebius shows that in early church history it was standard to interpret the words of Matthew 28:19 as a reference to baptism in the name of Jesus. This interpretation apparently began to change when the proponents of trinitarianism, which developed during the 200s and 300s, tried to find scriptural support for their position.

Harmony of Scripture

1. *Parallel passages.* Matthew was not the only writer to record the last instructions of Jesus to His disciples. Both Mark and Luke record equivalent teachings in somewhat different language (Mark 16:15-18;

Luke 24:47-49; Acts 1:4-8). Each account records Jesus' command to His disciples to preach the gospel everywhere and His promise that divine presence and power would accompany them. Matthew and Mark both mention baptism, and Luke refers to it indirectly. (Compare Luke 24:47 with Acts 2:38.)

Significantly, all three Gospel accounts describe a name in which the disciples are to proclaim the gospel. In each case, including Matthew, the name is singular. In Mark's account, Jesus said, "In my name" (Mark 16:17). Luke's account says repentance and remission of sins would be preached "in his name" (Luke 24:47). To harmonize Matthew with Mark and Luke, we must understand that "the name of the Father, and of the Son, and of the Holy Ghost" is Jesus.

2. *Fulfillment.* In the final analysis, the whole of Scripture is the context for interpreting a particular passage. When we study the Book of Acts and the Epistles, we find that the rest of the New Testament interprets Matthew 28:19 to be a reference to the name of Jesus. The apostles uniformly carried out the instructions of Jesus by baptizing in His name. They were the ones who heard the words of Jesus directly. They were able to integrate those words into His total teaching to a greater extent than we can today, and they had the opportunity to ask for a detailed explanation. Thus they were in the best position to interpret His meaning correctly and to obey His command exactly. Since the apostles understood and fulfilled the words of Jesus in Matthew 28:19 by baptizing everyone in the name

of Jesus, we should do the same today.

Significantly, this conclusion holds whether or not the doctrine of the trinity is correct. While some of the points we have made about Matthew 28:19 rest upon a nontrinitarian interpretation of the Bible, the arguments from grammar, context, and harmony of Scripture stand independent of a discussion of the Godhead. Consequently, many trinitarians recognize that the New Testament in general and Matthew 28:19 in particular teach baptism by invoking the name of Jesus Christ.[6]

Conclusion

Matthew 28:19 does not contradict the rest of Scripture; rather, it teaches the same truth as Acts and the Epistles. It describes the name of Jesus as the name in which to baptize. The proper way to understand, obey, and fulfill Matthew 28:19 is to follow the example of the apostles, the ones to whom Jesus personally gave the command. In short, we are not merely to repeat the words of Matthew 28:19 at baptism, but we are to invoke the name it describes—the name of Jesus.

7

The Baptismal Formula and the Greek Text

In Acts 2:38, the apostle Peter, with the support of the other apostles, commanded his Jewish audience to "be baptized every one of you in the name of Jesus Christ." Scripture records that the Samaritans, the Gentiles, and the disciples of John at Ephesus were also baptized in the name of Jesus Christ (Acts 8:16; 10:48; 19:5).

The Oneness Pentecostal movement understands these passages as descriptive of the baptismal formula. That is, we should actually invoke or utter the name of Jesus when baptizing a person. In response, some trinitarians argue that the phrase only means to baptize with Christ's authority and has no reference to the actual formula. A study of the original Greek text sheds considerable light upon this contention and assists in a clearer view of the significance of the name of Jesus in baptism.

The Exercise of Power and Authority

At the outset, we acknowledge that God's name represents His power and authority. Indeed, this explains the significance and importance of using Jesus' name in baptism. Baptism is part of salvation; it is for remission of sins (Acts 2:38; 22:16; I Peter 3:21). Jesus is the only saving name and the name in which sins are forgiven and remitted (Acts 4:12; 10:43; I John 2:12).

To baptize in Jesus' name is to baptize with His power and authority. But this does not imply that the name of Jesus should not be used. To the contrary, the proper way to act with God's authority and exercise His power is to invoke His name.

This is analogous to legal transactions then and now. A person has the power and authority to direct his bank to pay money from his account to whomever he designates. Yet the bank requires his signed name before it will honor his instruction. For someone to exercise the power of attorney for another, he must first present an appropriate document signed by the person he represents.

When David approached Goliath in the power and authority of God, He proclaimed, "I come to thee in the name of the LORD [Jehovah] of hosts" (I Samuel 17:45). David actually invoked the name of Jehovah.

Jesus gave the church power and authority to cast out demons in His name and to pray for the healing of the sick in His name (Mark 16:17-18; James 5:14). How did the New Testament church exercise this power and authority?

The apostle Peter declared to the lame man, "In the name of Jesus Christ of Nazareth rise up and walk" (Acts 3:6). He told the multitude, "And his name through faith in his name hath made this man strong" (Acts 3:16). Peter actually invoked the name of Jesus and also exercised faith in Jesus. He told the Jewish council that the man was healed "by the name of Jesus Christ of Nazareth" (Act 4:10), quoting the words he had used.

When Paul cast a demon out of a young woman, he said, "I command thee in the name of Jesus Christ to come out of her" (Acts 16:18). He called the name of Jesus. When the sons of Sceva sought to cast out demons, they said, "We adjure you by Jesus whom Paul preacheth" (Acts 19:13). They knew that Paul cast out demons by using the name of Jesus, so they attempted to do the same. They were unsuccessful because they did not have faith in Jesus or a genuine relationship with Him.

Whenever the early church exercised the power and authority of Jesus to obtain a spiritual work, they always invoked the name of Jesus in faith. Baptism for the remission of sins is no exception.

Invoking the Name

Theologians and church historians generally recognize that the Book of Acts gives the baptismal formula of the early church. The *Encyclopedia of Religion and Ethics* states, with respect to New Testament baptism, "The formula used was 'in the name of the Lord Jesus Christ' or some synonymous phrase; there is no evidence for the use of the trine name."[1] *The Interpreter's Dictionary* of the Bible says, "The evidence of Acts 2:38; 10:48 (cf. 8:16; 19:5), supported by Galatians 3:27, Romans 6:3, suggests that baptism in early Christianity was administered, not in the threefold name, but 'in the name of Jesus Christ' or 'in the name of the Lord Jesus.' "[2] Although he apparently used the threefold formula, Martin Luther defended people in his day who used "the words, 'I baptize you in the name of Jesus Christ,' " for he maintained, "It is certain the apostles used this formula in baptizing, as we read in the Acts of the Apostles."[3]

This is the natural reading of the phrase "baptized in the name of Jesus Christ," and a person must use questionable methods of biblical interpretation to deny that the words mean what they appear to mean. If this language were not a formula, it is strange that it appears so many times as if it were a formula without any explanation to the contrary.

Moreover, if this language does not describe a formula, then neither can a person appeal to Matthew 28:19 to find a formula. The Greek phrase translated as "in the name of" in Matthew 28:19 is identical to the phrase in Acts 8:16 and 19:5. If Acts tells us to exercise Christ's authority without a formula, then Matthew 28:19 says to exercise the authority of the Father, Son, and Holy Ghost without a formula. If this interpretation were correct, we would be left without any baptismal formula, which would be highly unlikely in light of the importance of baptism, the need to distinguish Christian baptism from other types of baptism, the common-sense reading of the passages in question, and the historical evidence from the earliest times that Christians always used a baptismal formula.

In addition to the baptismal accounts in Acts 2, 8, 10, and 19, the Epistles allude to the baptismal formula in the name of Jesus (Romans 6:3-4; I Corinthians 1:13; 6:11; Galatians 3:27; Colossians 2:12). Properly interpreted, Matthew 28:19 describes the name of Jesus. Moreover, Acts 15:17, Acts 22:16, and James 2:7 indicate that the name of Jesus was orally invoked at baptism.

These last three verses use the Greek verb *epikaleo*, which is composed of the preposition *epi* and the verb *kaleo*. *Kaleo* simply means to call. *Epi* has a variety of uses, but its most basic and literal meaning is "on, in, above, answering the question 'where?' "[4] Thus *epikaleo* means to invoke, call, call on, or call upon.

Acts 15:17 describes the Gentiles whom God has chosen as those "upon whom my name is called." The verb is *epikaleo* in perfect passive form. The passive voice means the action was done to the people spoken about. The Greek perfect tense means the action took place in the past but has present and continuing effects. Acts 15:17 also uses the preposition *epi* separately. This double use of *epi* stresses the idea of invocation on or upon.

God's name was called over or invoked upon the Gentile converts, and as a result they still bear His name. Marshall's *Interlinear Greek-English New Testament* gives the literal translation: "on whom has been invoked the name of me." A number of other translations emphasize the specific act of invocation, some focusing on the past event and others upon the present result: "upon whom my name has been invoked" (Amplified and Berkeley); "upon whom my name is called" (Phillips); "who bear my name" (NIV).

James 2:7 also uses the verb *epikaleo* followed by the preposition *epi*: "Do not they blaspheme that worthy name by the which ye are called?" Again, a specific act of invocation is indicated: "called on you" (Marshall); "which was invoked over you" (RSV); "which hath been invoked upon you" (Rotherham). Here, the form of the verb is aorist passive participle. The aorist tense denotes simple past action, while the aorist participle means the action occurred prior to the time of the main verb, which is present tense.

Acts 15:17 and James 2:7, then, point to a specific time in the past when God's name was invoked over each believer. When did this occur? And what name was used? The New Testament records only one event in which the divine name is orally invoked over each Christian—at the act of water baptism. And the only name that appears in connection with water baptism is the name of Jesus Christ.

This conclusion is so clear that the translators of *The Amplified Bible,* although they were of the trinitarian persuasion, felt compelled to translate James 2:7 with an explanation in brackets: "Is it not they who slander and blaspheme that precious name by which you are distinguished and called [the name of Christ invoked in baptism]?"

Some interpret Acts 15:17 and James 2:7 as symbolic only, referring to God's ownership of the saint and the saint's dedication to God. W. E. Vine says the verb in these two verses means "to be called by a person's name; hence it is used of being declared to be dedicated to a person."[5] This reveals the significance of invoking the name but does not obviate the actual invocation. As Walter Bauer et al. explain both verses, "Someone's name is called over someone to designate the latter as the property of the former."[6]

Acts 22:16 confirms that an actual invocation of the name of Jesus occurs at the conversion experience, namely, at water baptism: "Arise, and be baptized, and wash away thy sins, calling on the name of the Lord." The verb *epikaleo* appears here as well, indicating a specific invocation: "invoking the name of him" (Marshall); "while invoking his name (Jerusalem Bible); "with invocation of his name" (NEB); "by calling upon His name" (Amplified); "and invoke his name" (TCNT); "as you call on his name" (Phillips); "by calling on His name" (Williams). According to Vine, in Acts 22:16 the verb means "to call upon for oneself," while another form of the same verb in Acts 2:21 means "to call upon by way of adoration, making use of the Name of the Lord."[7] Of these two verses Bauer et al. say the verb is used to "call upon someone for aid . . . calling on a divinity."[8]

Using the Name of Jesus

Acts 2:38, 8:16, 10:48, and 19:5 all teach baptism in the name of Jesus. Some trinitarians reject the idea that these four verses speak of a formula, basing their argument on the slight variations in the wording. For example, Acts 2:38 says, "Jesus Christ," while Acts 8:16 and 19:5 say, "Lord Jesus."

But their reasoning is faulty. What is significant is that in the Greek all four verses include the name Jesus. Since the titles vary in the four passages but the name of Jesus is used consistently, the implication is that it is not the title that is so important but the vital element to make baptism valid is the name of Jesus.

In the King James Version, Acts 10:48 says, "In the name of the Lord." The name of the Lord is Jesus, for the earliest confession of the Christian church was, "Jesus is Lord." (See Romans 10:9; I Corinthians 12:3; Philippians 2:11.) Moreover, the evidence is strong that the original Greek text of Acts 10:48 actually states, "In the name of Jesus Christ," and all translations since the KJV (except the NKJV) use the name of Jesus.

"In the name of Jesus Christ" appears in the

The Baptismal Formula and the Greek Text

Bodmer Papyri; five major uncials (the most ancient manuscripts, written in all capitals), including the Sinaiticus, Alexandrinus, and Vaticanus; ten major miniscules (later manuscripts written with small letters); a major lectionary (an ancient collection of Scripture readings for church services); five ancient versions (Old Latin, Vulgate, Syriac, Coptic, and Armenian); and three ancient writers (the author of the *Treatise on Rebaptism,* Cyril of Jerusalem, and John Chrysostom).[9] Other variations that include the name Jesus occur in another major uncial (Ephraemi Rescriptus), three major miniscules, the majority of lectionaries, the Georgian version, and some manuscripts of the Byzantine tradition. By contrast, the reading of "Lord" by itself occurs only in one major uncial, three lesser uncials, nine major miniscules, three major lectionaries, and some of the Byzantine manuscripts.

An illuminating fact emerges from a study of the Greek text of Acts 2:38, 8:16, 10:48, and 19:5. In each of these verses, the KJV says, "In the name," using the same preposition *in*, but the Greek text uses three different prepositions: *epi* with the dative case, *eis* with the accusative, and *en* with the dative.

Acts 2:38 uses *epi* with the dative. It says, *epi to onomati Iesou Christou,* literally, "on (or in) the name of Jesus Christ." According to *A Greek-English Lexicon of the New Testament* by Bauer, Arndt, Gingrich, and Danker, which is the most highly respected Greek-English dictionary for the New Testament, this means "when someone's name is mentioned or called upon, or mentioning someone's name."[10] For example, this phrase describes the false teachers who use Christ's name (Matthew 24:5; Mark 13:6; Luke 21:8) and the apostles when they spoke and taught using Jesus' name (Acts 4:17, 18; 5:28, 40). It also appears in Luke 24:47. *The Interpreter's Dictionary of the Bible* notes that it "gives the sense of resting upon, or being devoted to, the person of Christ."[11]

Acts 8:16 and 19:5 use *eis*, which indicates "motion into a thing or into its immediate vicinity . . . of place, into, in, toward."[12] The phrase here is *eis to onoma tou kuriou Iesou*, and it literally means, "into the name of the Lord Jesus." Bauer et al. explain its significance: "Through baptism . . . the one who is baptized becomes the possession of and comes under the protection of the one whose name he bears; he is under the control of the effective power of the name and the One who bears the name, i.e., he is dedicated to them . . . . An additional factor, to a degree, may be the sense of . . . 'with mention of the name.' "[13] Matthew 28:19 also uses *eis*.

Acts 10:48 uses the preposition *en*, which literally means "in, of the space within which something is found."[14] The verse reads *en to onomati Iesou Christou*. According to Bauer et al., "*en onomati* of God or Jesus means in the great majority of cases with mention of the name, while naming or calling on the name. . . . In many pass[ages] it seems to be a formula."[15] As examples, they cite it as an utterance or formula in casting out demons (Mark 9:38; 16:17; Luke 9:49; 10:17) and praying for healing (Acts 3:6; 4:7, 10). Acts 16:18 is another such example.

Bauer et al. give further examples where this phrase means to mention the name, providing these translations: "be baptized or have oneself baptized while naming the name of Jesus Christ" (Acts 10:48); "ask the Father, using my name" (John 15:16); "(the Father) will give you, when you mention my name" (John 16:23); anoint the sick with oil "while calling on the name of the Lord" (James 5:14); "that when the name of Jesus is mentioned every knee should bow" (Philippians 2:10).[16] In I Corinthians 6:11, which is a reference to baptism, and in John 20:31, they say the phrase means "through or by the name . . . the effect brought about by the name is caused by the utterance of the name."[17] Colossians 3:17 also uses *en*. *The Interpreter's Dictionary of the Bible* says *en* "conveys the idea of acting on the authority of another" but also can mean " 'by invoking the name'—i.e., while calling upon Christ."[18]

F. F. Bruce, the dean of twentieth-century evangelical scholars, similarly concluded from a study of the Greek prepositions that Matthew 28:19 may be a symbolic reference but that Acts 2:38 probably refers specifically to the invocation of the name of Jesus at water baptism:

> While *en to onomati* or *epi to onomati* means "in (or 'with') the name" or "on the authority" of someone, I suggest that *eis to onoma* implies a

transference of ownership, as when we to-day speak of paying money "into someone's name." This is noteworthy in the baptismal formulae of the New Testament: baptism "into the name" of the Triune God (Matt. 28:19), or "into the name of the Lord Jesus" (Acts 8:16; 19:5; cf. I Cor. 1:13, 15), is the sign that he is Lord and that the baptised person belongs to him; baptism "in the name of Jesus Christ" (Acts 2:38; 10:48) probably refers to the pronouncing of his name by the baptiser (cf. Jas. 2:7; Acts 15:17) or the invoking of his name by the baptised person (Acts 22:16).[19]

In conclusion, the New Testament teaches that water baptism should be performed in the name of Jesus, typically adding the title of Lord or Christ or both to identify the Lord Jesus Christ specifically. As a study of the Greek text confirms, baptism in the name of Jesus means to invoke the name of Jesus orally upon the candidate. In this way, we express our faith in Jesus, our reliance upon His saving work, our devotion to Him, our entrance into His body (the church), and our exercise of His authority. The believer who repents and is baptized in the name of the Lord Jesus Christ relies upon the power and authority of Jesus Christ for the remission of sins and dedicates himself to Jesus Christ as his Lord.

NOTES

Chapter 2. The Significance of God's Name

[1] R. Abba, "Name," *The Interpreter's Dictionary of the Bible* [hereinafter *IDB*], George Buttrick et. al, eds. (Nashville: Abingdon, 1962), 3:500-1.

[2] B. W. Anderson, *IDB*, 2:407.

[3] Abba, *IDB*, 3:501-3.

[4] Ibid., 3:501, 506.

Chapter 3. Call His Name Jesus

[1] W. E. Vine, *An Expository Dictionary of New Testament Words* (Old Tappan, NJ: Revell, 1940), 274; Marvin Vincent, *Word Studies in the New Testament* (Rpt. Grand Rapids: Eerdmans, 1975), 1:16.

[2] Henry Flanders, Jr. and Bruce Cresson, *Introduction to the Bible* (New York: John Wiley and Sons, 1973), 79.

Chapter 5. Baptism in the Name of Jesus

[1] Walter Bauer, W. F. Arndt, F. W. Gingrich, and Frederick Danker, *A Greek-English Lexicon of the New Testament,* 2nd ed. (Chicago: University of Chicago Press, 1979), 572.

Chapter 6. The Baptismal Formula according to Matthew 28:19

[1] Matthew Henry, *Commentary* (Old Tappan, NJ:

Revell, n.d.), 5:443.
 ²G. R. Beasley-Murray, *Baptism in the New Testament* (Grand Rapids: Eerdmans, 1962), 83, emphasis in original.
 ³Ibid., 83-84.
 ⁴Ibid., 81.
 ⁵R. V. G. Tasker, *The Gospel According to St. Matthew*, vol. 1 of *The Tyndale New Testament Commentaries* (Grand Rapids: Eerdmans, 1961), 275.
 ⁶See James Lee Beall, *Rise to Newness of Life* (Detroit: Evangel Press, 1974), 60-62; J. David Pawson, *The Normal Christian Birth* (London: Hodder & Stoughton, 1989), 93-99.

Chapter 7. The Baptismal Formula and the Greek Text

¹Kirsopp Lake, "Baptism (Early Christian)," *Encyclopedia of Religion and Ethics,* James Hastings, ed. (New York: Charles Scribner's Sons, 1951), 2:384.
 ²W. F. Flemington, "Baptism," *IDB*, 1:351.
 ³Martin Luther, "The Babylonian Captivity of the Church," in *Word and Sacrament II,* vol. 36 of *Luther's Works,* ed. Abdel Wentz (Philadelphia: Muhlenberg Press, 1959), 63.
 ⁴Bauer et al., 286.
 ⁵W. E. Vine, 165.
 ⁶Bauer et al., 294.
 ⁷Vine, 166.
 ⁸Bauer et al., 294.
 ⁹Kurt Aland et al., eds., *The Greek New Testament,* 3d ed. (Stuttgart, W. Ger.: United Bible Societies, 1983), 458-59.
 ¹⁰Bauer et al., 573.
 ¹¹Abba, *IDB*, 3:507.

[12]Bauer et al., 228.
[13]Ibid., 572.
[14]Ibid., 258.
[15]Ibid., 572.
[16]Ibid.
[17]Ibid., 573.
[18]Abba, *IDB*, 3:507.
[19]F. F. Bruce, *The Books and the Parchments,* rev. ed. (Old Tappan, NJ: Revell, 1984), 57 n.20.

* * * * * *

For further discussion of the doctrine of God, including various titles of God, see David Bernard, *The Oneness of God* (Hazelwood, MO: Word Aflame Press, 1983).

For further discussion of water baptism, see David Bernard, *The New Birth* (Hazelwood, MO: Word Aflame Press, 1983).

Works by David K. Bernard

Books:
Series in Pentecostal Theology
    Volume 1 – *The Oneness of God*
    Volume 2 – *The New Birth*
    Volume 3 – *In Search of Holiness*
            (with Loretta Bernard)
    Volume 4 – *Practical Holiness: A Second Look*
Handbook of Basic Doctrines
Essential Doctrines of the Bible (booklet)
Essentials of Oneness Theology (booklet)
Essentials of the New Birth (booklet)
Essentials of the New Birth – Spanish (booklet)
Essentials of Holiness (booklet)
A Study Guide for the New Birth (with Neil Stegall)
A Study Guide for the Oneness of God (with Neil Stegall)
The Message of Romans
The Message of Colossians and Philemon
Oneness and Trinity, A.D. 100–300

Tape Series:
Holiness Seminar
Oneness Revival
Highlights from Romans

NOTES

NOTES

NOTES

NOTES

NOTES

NOTES

NOTES

NOTES